All About Your Canary

Contents

Introduction

As their name suggests, canaries were originally found on the Canary Islands off the African Coast. They are members of the finch family, which contains thousands of other species, but their enchanting song and their adaptability as a pet led to their rapid domestication. In fact, many varieties of canary that are not found in the wild have been bred in captivity.

Canaries are relatively cheap to purchase, easy to keep, and are generally hardy and resistant to disease. Despite this, like any species of animal that is kept as a pet, it is essential to think carefully about their requirements before you purchase them, and to understand how best to keep them.

Birds kept properly are not only likely to be happier and healthier, but they are also much more rewarding. If you are looking for a basic guide to provide the information you need to care for canaries in a domestic environment, then this is the book for you.

DID YOU KNOW?

Border Fancy Canaries were originally known as Cumberland Canaries in England but as Common Canaries in Scotland. This caused a major difference of opinion, but at a meeing in Cumbria in 1890, a peaceful solution was finally reached when the new name was adopted internationally.

Different Types

There are three main types of canary: the Roller Canary, which has been bred for its song, and where appearance is not important; the Colour Bred types that can be found in a wide range of colours, and where the plumage is considered the most important feature; and those bred for other characteristics such as size or unusual shape. Feather types are referred to as 'Buff' or 'Yellow', which does not relate to the colour, but to the nature of the feathers themselves, which are larger and coarser in buff birds.

The sociable canary is happiest living with other birds.

Understanding Canaries

Although canaries are all a delight to watch and listen to, they will not generally form a close bond with their owner in the same way as members of the parrot family, such as the budgerigar. With patience, they can be trained so that they will hop on to a finger placed in front of them.

Canaries are often kept individually, but they are happiest living with other birds. They are quite timid, and should not be subjected to sudden, loud noises or flashing lights, nor should they be housed with more aggressive birds such as budgies and parakeets.

Canary Varieties

Roller Canary

This breed is indisputably the best singing canary of all. The cock bird keeps his beak almost closed when singing, but adopts an upright stance and holds his head raised. Variegated yellow colours are most common, but plumage is not considered important for show purposes, as birds are judged mainly on their operatic abilities.

Variegated Buff Border Canary.

Border Fancy Canary

This breed was developed on the borders of England and Scotland towards the end of the 19th century. They are hardy birds that can be kept in an outdoor aviary throughout the year and are ideal for beginners.

The plumage should be a characteristic 'canary yellow', but may be variegated, with patches of white or brown. White, cinnamon, and green colour variations have also been bred. They are fairly large with a well-rounded head and body. The Fife variation is similar in appearance but smaller in size.

Fawn and White Fife canary.

Gloster Fancy Canary

This relative newcomer has been produced by crossing crested Roller Canaries with small Border Fancy Canaries, in the English county of Gloucester. They have become very popular since the Second World War.

This variety normally has a combination of light and dark plumage and a small, stocky body. Crested head feathers, which should not grow down to cover the eyes, give the appearance of a bird that has had a 'pudding-basin' hair-cut.

Buff Corona Gloster Canary.

Red Factor Canary

In the 1920s, domestic canaries were crossed with Blackhooded Red Siskins (another member of the finch family) with the aim of producing red canaries. Colour intensity is all-important for show birds, which may vary depending on the bird's diet. Special diets are available to encourage the development of the red colouring and avoid an undesirable orange tinge.

Red Factor Canary.

Canary Varieties

Yorkshire Fancy Canary

This breed was developed in the Yorkshire coalfields in northern England in the 1860s, when birds were taken down the mines to help detect poisonous gases. They are slim birds that are easy to keep, but can be tricky to breed in captivity.

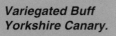

Variegated Buff Yorkshire Canary.

Lizard Canary

Probably the oldest surviving breed of canary, they are bred for their distinctive plumage. The body should be silky in appearance, with crescent-shaped markings on the back, and with lines on the side of the body called 'rowings'. The feet and legs should be darkly coloured. The multi-coloured body contrasts with a yellow 'cap' of feathers on the head. They are hardy birds that are easy to keep indoors or out.

Scotch Fancy Canary

This is one of the 'type' breeds that has been bred for its unusual shape, probably from the Belgian Fancy Canary. The bird has an obvious curve to its long body, holding its head bent forward over its long neck, and its elongated tail curved under its perch. It also has a characteristic hopping movement from perch to perch, jumping and turning without the use of its wings.

It is a specialised breed that is becoming more widely available after a decrease in popularity earlier this century.

Diamorphic Belgian Canaries.

Unlike many of the larger species of birds, canaries are sufficiently small to be kept satisfactorily in a cage, so long as it is spacious enough for them to fly around freely. Ideally, they should also be given free space to exercise. An indoor aviary makes an excellent home, but it is also possible to keep most varieties in outdoor aviaries, providing there is appropriate shelter.

DID YOU KNOW?

Canaries, like all other members of the finch family, use three toes to grip the perch in front, and one behind, whereas psittacines such as parrots and budgerigars use two feet in front of the perch and two behind.

The Cage

A rectangular cage about 20 ins (48 cms) in length is fine for one or two birds. Cages can be made either of wire-mesh, with a plastic base, or of a wooden box construction with a wire-mesh front. Avoid those that are primarily decorative and do not allow enough space for the birds to fly around.

Purchase your cage and have it set up and fully equipped before you acquire your birds, so that it is ready for them to settle into as soon as they arrive home.

A cage must be big enough so your canary can fly.

Match Making

If you want to tame a bird, you should keep only one, but be prepared to give it plenty of attention. Hen birds can be paired together, but will not usually sing, and cock birds will fight if they are kept in the same cage.

As there are no externally visible physical differences between male and female canaries, choosing the sex will be largely a matter of chance, although as they mature the cock bird can be distinguished by his singing ability. Many people like to keep one canary with other species of finch – budgerigars will usually intimidate them.

White Fife Canaries: Plan accommodation before buying your birds.

Setting Up Home

Locating The Cage

Position the cage away from any heat source, such as a radiator, and away from any draughts. Direct sunlight is often enjoyed by canaries, but they may overheat if they are unable to find shade, so ensure part of the cage is covered for protection. The kitchen is not a good place for a canary cage due to the extreme fluctuations of temperature and the fumes that occur when cooking is underway.

DID YOU KNOW?

Birds are very susceptible to poisoning by fumes, which is why miners used to take canaries down the mines. They should be removed from the room if there is a lot of cigarette smoke or an open fire. Even the fumes from an over-heated, non-stick saucepan can be highly toxic to a pet bird.

Equipment

Lining the cage:
Special sanded sheets are available for lining the floor of the cage so that droppings and discarded seed husks can be cleaned away every few days.

Perches:
A variety of perches is important. These should be made of softwood, and must be wide enough so that the bird's feet only wrap about three-quarters of the way around them. Natural branches from a fruit tree are ideal, providing they have not been sprayed with pesticide.

Toys:
Canaries do not 'work out' with toys to the same extent as a bird such as a budgie, but a small swing and

one or two items such as a table-tennis ball or a mirror are often appreciated.

Water-bottle:
A fresh supply of water is essential, and it is best to provide this with a gravity-fed water-bottle.

Feeding bowl:
If you are keeping more than one canary, make sure they each have a feeding bowl.

Cage cover:
A cage cover will prevent the birds from being startled if the lights are turned on suddenly at night.

Buying A Canary

L̲ate October/November is the best time to buy a bird, as the breeding season will be over and there should be a good selection of young adult stock to choose from. Most pet stores will supply canaries, but make sure you go to a reputable shop that has knowledgeable staff, and where the birds are well-kept. You could go to a recognised breeder, and they will often be happy to sell on birds that are unsuitable for showing and breeding, but that will make perfect pets.

Watch the birds from a distance before making your choice.

Making Your Choice

Watch the birds in their cage quietly from a distance before choosing. Avoid the bird that sits with its feathers fluffed up, asleep on its perch when the others are jumping around. Healthy birds usually sleep with just one foot grasping the perch, so be on guard if a bird is having to use both to keep its grip, particularly if its head is drooped forwards.

Settling In

Any bird is likely to be off-colour and unsettled for a few days after a move to a new environment, but a reputable dealer should always be prepared to give you a refund if a bird becomes ill soon after purchase.

If you already have some birds in a group, always try to keep any newcomers in isolation for at least two weeks before introducing them. Even a bird that seems perfectly healthy could be incubating a disease that may be passed on to the others. Do not integrate the newcomers until you are confident that they are not showing any signs of ill health (see page 26).

(see page 26)

SIGNS OF A HEALTHY CANARY

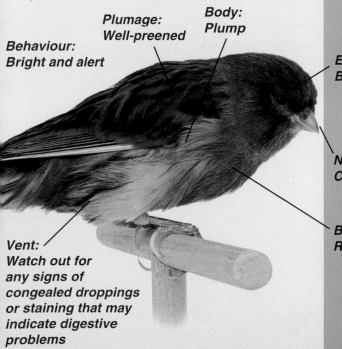

Behaviour: Bright and alert

Plumage: Well-preened

Body: Plump

Eyes: Bright

Nostrils: Clean

Breathing: Rapid but quiet

Vent: Watch out for any signs of congealed droppings or staining that may indicate digestive problems

Feeding Your Canary

Members of the finch family eat mainly seeds, especially the grasses. In the wild, canaries would eat seedling plants such as cabbage and lettuce, and canary grass. 'Canary seed' is an important part of any canary food that is commercially available.

Seed Mixes

Commercial seed mixes may contain half a dozen different types of seed, but when fed ad lib, many canaries will only pick out their favourites. This can result in an unbalanced diet, but the effect can be minimised by restricting the daily ration to the bird's needs, so that it will eat the complete mixture.

A canary will need about two level teaspoons of seeds per day, but this may need to be varied depending up the size and activity of the bird. If there is more than one canary in the cage, separate dishes should be used for each bird to ensure those at the bottom of the 'pecking order' get their ration.

Canary seed.

A canary's diet is based on seeds.

14

Fruit And Vegetables

Fruits, vegetables and greens should account for about a quarter of the diet. They must be washed thoroughly to remove chemicals and be cut into small chunks. They should be offered in a separate dish to the seed mixture.

Grit

In the wild, a bird would naturally consume grit as it pecks around for its food to aid in the mechanical digestion of seeds and nuts. Provide some fine grit in a separate bowl so that your canaries can take some in if they choose. Commercially available products are specially designed to provide essential minerals within the grit.

Grit is an essential aid to digestion.

Cuttlefish Bone

Cuttlebones, the internal shell of the cuttlefish, are also appreciated as a source of calcium. They need to be soaked in water for a couple of days to remove excess salt.

Egg-Food

Canaries seem to need and enjoy having small amounts of scrambled egg or store-bought 'Egg food' as a source of animal protein a couple times weekly.

Egg-food is a good source of protein

Feeding Your Canary

Insects

Some people will offer their bird insects occasionally, and although good for the canary, this may be rather distasteful for owners.

Mash

A wide range of crumble or mash diets, designed to provide for different stages of a canary's life, can be purchased, and these are generally an excellent food source.

Water

Although most canaries do not drink a lot, a supply of clean, fresh water should always be available.

Tasty Treats For Canaries

Here are some of the goodies that you can let your birds enjoy in small quantities from time to time:

Banana should be an occasional treat.

- Apple
- Banana
- Lettuce
- Spinach
- Watercress
- Dandelion leaves (ensure any weeds have not been treated with herbicides)
- Celery
- Peas
- Egg biscuit
- Milk-soaked bread.

Dandelion leaves.

Spinach and other greens must be washed before feeding.

16

A recipe for canary high protein food

- Take a hard-boiled egg and mash the white and the yolk together
- Add one teaspoonful of Brewer's yeast
- Add a pinch of powdered avian vitamin supplement
- Mix well.

Offer only small quantities of this food, and remove any uneaten remnants before they have a chance to go off.

This can be put into a feeding bowl and left in the cage for 24 hours, after which time it should be discarded. It is great for giving that extra boost when birds are stressed, such as during moulting or when laying eggs.

Supplements

Healthy birds that are being fed a varied diet, should not need a supplement to their food. However, at times of stress such as moulting or breeding, you could add a balanced vitamin and mineral supplement to a moist food.

Gloster Black-capped Buff Corona.

Many canaries enjoy being fed seed that has been soaked in water for a day or two and then rinsed off, and powdered supplements will adhere to this much better than to dry seed.

Handling And Training

There may be times when you need to handle a canary – for example, if it needs to have its nails trimmed (see Page 21), its leg bands checked (see Page 21), or you may need to transport a canary to the vet or to a show. The best method is to gently grasp the body in one hand. The hold should be firm but not so tight as to squeeze the bird.

Finger-taming: The canary must become accustomed to your hand in the cage.

Finger-Training

If you want to finger-train a bird, you should start when it is as young as possible. With patience, a canary will gradually become used to human company and will readily perch on a finger and eat seed out of the palm of the hand. Once they become finger-tame, they can be allowed

With patience, a canary will learn to perch on your finger.

18

out of their cage to exercise, which gives them a great deal more freedom.

Competitions

For competitions, Roller Canaries are taught to sing set pieces, called tours and rolls -- from which comes its name. The song can range over nearly three octaves and is particularly pure-sounding and melodic.

New birds used to be taught by an older bird, but, nowadays, it is possible to get hold of cassette tapes specifically designed to do the job. If you are keen to develop the singing talents of your bird, you need to keep two male birds in the same room to encourage them to compete with each other. However, they must be housed in separate cages or fighting will break out. You can get more information on competitions from a Canary Club in your area.

The male canary is the superior of the sexes when it comes to singing.

Caring For Your Canary

Canaries need to have their cage cleaned out regularly. The litter or sand sheet on the floor of the cage needs to be changed when it becomes soiled. Fine grit suitable for canaries is also available commercially. Empty seed husks and uneaten perishable food need to be removed, the dishes cleaned, and the water changed.

Once a week the cage needs a more thorough clean, with all furnishings and toys removed and washed, and the bars of the cage wiped over with a damp cloth.

You are responsible for your canary's health and well-being.

Moulting

Canaries normally moult in the late summer over a period of about six weeks, which can cause them some stress and put a cock bird off his singing. Prolonged or repeated moulting may be due to the bird being kept at too high a temperature.

Canaries enjoy bathing regularly, and a bowl of water for splashing should be provided. Some canaries prefer being sprayed with an fine atomiser of lukewarm water on a daily basis, especially when moulting.

Canaries enjoy a regular bath.

Nails

If the perches are of a suitable diameter and the bird has access to a cuttlefish bone, the beak and nails should wear down naturally and never need clipping. Overgrown nails may interfere with the bird's ability to perch properly, and will be obvious if they are twisting out at abnormal angles.

The nails can be clipped by holding them up to the light to see the pink quick that runs down the middle of the nail, and leaving about an eighth of an inch above that. Ordinary nail-clippers can be used for the task. Be careful not to cut the nail too short, as this may cause the bird some temporary discomfort and it may bleed for a while. If you are new to bird-keeping, ask an expert to help.

DID YOU KNOW?

Canaries can become sexually mature from just three months of age.

Identification

If you want to show your canaries, or to breed from canaries kept in groups, you will need to permanently identify them. This is normally done with special, coloured, metal bands, known as closed rings, each engraved with the bird's own number. These can be slipped over the leg when the chicks are between four and seven days of age.

A leg-band is used for identification.

Alternatively, a plastic 'open ring' can be applied when the bird is older with the help of a special tool. Again, this is a job for an expert.

The birds that you purchase may already be banded, and you should check the bands from time to time to ensure they are still moving freely on the leg. If dirt gets trapped in them, they can make the leg inflamed and swollen, and even cut off the blood supply to the foot.

Leaving Your Canary

Canaries should not be left without supervision for more than a day or two as they need their food topped up regularly, and empty husks need to be cleared away. The birds must also be checked to ensure they are not showing any signs of being unwell. A small cage is easy to transport, so you can always take your canary to a friend rather than having someone to come in regularly to visit. Leave clear written instructions of your canary's requirements and details of your vet, if relevant.

On The Move

You are likely to need to transport your canary occasionally, at least to a veterinary surgery if it is unwell. A small travelling cage is ideal, but a cardboard box will do for a short journey. Some people take their pet birds on holiday with them, which is fine in a caravan or self-catering accommodation, but they must not be left in excessively hot temperatures for any length of time, or they can suffer from heat-stroke. A water-spray can help to keep the bird cool during a particularly hot journey.

Breeding

Although it is not unusual for experienced bird-keepers to breed canaries in a home environment, they are not the easiest of pet birds to breed. The increasing day length in March will usually stimulate canaries to breed, and mating usually occurs during the spring, so potential breeding pairs should be matched together in December.

It takes considerable experience to breed canaries successfully.

One month prior to breeding, the hen should be introduced to soft, high-energy foods. Commercial rearing and conditioning foods are available for this purpose. This diet will help bring her into tip-top condition, and will help her to cope with the demands of egg-laying and rearing her chicks.

Mating And Nesting

There are often no externally visible signs between cocks and hens. This is a Gloster Fawn Corona hen.

Canarie's nests are not covered, and so a nesting pan, made of ceramic or earthenware and lined with some soft felt, is generally provided. Ideally, the breeding pair should be moved into a wooden nesting box with a wire mesh front, separated by a solid partition that can be removed when both birds are judged to be ready for mating.

The female will respond to the male's frantic mating calls and courtship display by crouching low on the perch with her tail raised. She should then be provided with nesting material such as hay, moss, long grass or raffia, or even small strips of hessian sacking. The cock can remain with the hen to help rear the chicks, but some prove troublesome and these males are best removed after mating.

A Gloster Buff Corona Cock.

Egg-Laying

The female will develop a swelling on the underside of the tail near her vent opening when she is about to lay an egg (this can happen even in the absence of a male). Her feathers may become ruffled and her abdomen bloated, and she will lay from two to six eggs – usually one every day or two. The last egg is slightly darker in colour.

The Chicks

The young hatch after about fourteen days of incubation. For the first few days, they may eat very little, using up their reserves of yolk, but they then start to eat food regurgitated by their parents. They are not able to break the husks of hard seeds until they are about six weeks of age, so they are dependent upon the assistance of their parents until then. Their feathers appear at about three weeks of age.

Bird-keepers often remove the eggs from the hen until the whole clutch has been laid, and then return them for the hen to incubate.

Health Care

It is important to recognise any signs of ill health at an early stage, as prompt diagnosis and treatment is more likely to lead to a full recovery. Check the following:

Behaviour: Normally alert and inquisitive, a sick canary will be depressed, disinterested in its surroundings, and go off its food.

Feathers: Sleek and well-preened in a healthy bird, they become ruffled and untidy if the bird is unwell.

Body condition: Normal plumpness may be lost, and a hollowing of the muscles either side of the breast bone may be felt.

Vent: A single opening common to the digestive, urinary and reproductive tracts, it is normally clean, but may become sore and caked with droppings.

Eyes: Should be bright and clear. They may become dull or inflamed.

Breathing: May become laboured, possibly with a discharge from the nostrils.

Feet: May become swollen, or the canary may only perch on one leg.

Close observation is the key to ensuring that your canary is in good health.

Nursing A Sick Bird

Small birds have a very high metabolic rate, so they will rapidly use up their fat reserves and become very weak unless disease problems are identified quickly. If you have more than one bird, isolate the sick one, and keep it in a cage somewhere really warm until you can get it to a vet.

Warmth is a very important part of nursing sick canaries, as it will increase their resistance to disease considerably. It may be advisable to invest in a small infra-red heat lamp that can be suspended above the cage, but birds in that cage should be able to get out of the light if they feel they are getting too warm. You should aim for a temperature of about 90 degrees Fahrenheit (32 degrees Centigrade), and gradually reacclimatize the bird to a more normal temperature once it has recovered.

Medication

Getting medication into a sick canary is not easy. Some antibiotics come in the form of a soluble powder that can be added to the drinking water, but it can be difficult to ensure enough is taken. Medicated seed is an excellent way of administering drugs if the bird is eating.

Drops can be given directly into the mouth, but the physical handling necessary to administer the medication can sometimes cause the bird to go into shock and die, particularly if it is already stressed.

Treatment

Treating a bird as small as a canary is a challenging task, and very often the best that can be done is to examine the conditions under which the birds are kept, as a great deal of illness is due to poor husbandry.

If you do start to lose birds, arrange for a post-mortem examination to be carried out to discover the underlying disease. Small birds will die very quickly, only showing external signs of starvation once they stop eating, regardless of the cause.

Most veterinary surgeries will happily treat pet birds on an occasional basis, but if you have a difficult problem, you could ask to be referred on to a veterinary surgeon with a specialised interest in avian disease.

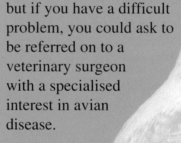

DID YOU KNOW?

Canaries prefer their cages to be situated as far as possible from the ground, because in the wild a predatory bird will attack from above.

Common Ailments

Digestive Disorders

If your bird's droppings are very
watery, an abnormal colour, or
even tinged with blood, this
could be due to enteritis, which
is an inflammation of the bowel.
A sudden change of diet may
bring about the condition, and
mild cases may settle down with
a change back to just plain seed.

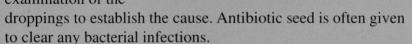

More severe diarrhoea may be due
to an infection, and
sometimes a vet
may need to carry
out a laboratory
examination of the
droppings to establish the cause. Antibiotic seed is often given
to clear any bacterial infections.

Parasites such as roundworms and tapeworms may also
show up on a faecal examination, and can cause loss of
condition and loose droppings. Liquid worming medication is
available for birds.

Sour Crop

Sour crop is a term given to an infection of the sac which is
used to store the seed after it has been swallowed, and will
cause the bird to keep regurgitating foul-smelling food. A
dilute solution (2 per cent) of antiseptic in the drinking water
may clear the problem, but antibiotics from a vet are often
needed.

A diet that is deficient in green vegetables may result in
constipation.

Common Ailments

Egg Binding

Female birds will often lay eggs even in the absence of a mate, although they will obviously be infertile. Removing the eggs will simply encourage her to lay more to replace them, so leaving them for her to try to incubate may be best.

Sometimes an egg becomes stuck inside the hen, which will cause her to strain to try pass it out. It may be visible just inside the cloaca. Extra warmth alone may relax her enough to allow her to pass the egg. Veterinary assistance is sometimes necessary to try to clear the egg, breaking up the egg and removing it piece by piece, or even attempting to remove it surgically.

There is a suggestion that nutritional imbalances may play an important part in causing egg binding, particularly the levels of calcium, vitamin A and vitamin D in the diet. If egg binding is a regular problem, check that the diet you are feeding is correctly balanced.

Respiratory Infections

There are several causes of respiratory infections in pet canaries, causing noisy and laboured breathing, often with a bubbly discharge from the nostrils. Prompt treatment, with appropriate medication by a veterinary surgeon, is essential as the condition can often be fatal.

Sore Feet

Perches of the wrong diameter can play a part in causing the problem, and obesity will obviously aggravate it by putting more weight on the feet, so the patient will need to cut down on fattening foods such as millet. Changing the perches and ensuring they are kept scrupulously clean may cure the problem, but sometimes antibiotic treatment is needed.

Wounds

These can be caused by fighting between birds, or injuries sustained within the cage or while flying. Flesh wounds can be bathed in a mild antiseptic solution daily until they heal, but must be watched closely for signs of infection.